LOVE IS

A FORMER MAGISTRATE'S POETIC
REFLECTIONS ON LOVE AND
MARRIAGE IN A COUNTY
COURTHOUSE

J. Anton Davis

All Points Creative, LLC

Published by All Points Creative, LLC.

All of the poems contained in this collection describe actual events witnessed by author J. Anton Davis while he served as a North Carolina Magistrate Judge. All of the events described in this book took place in a courtroom that was at all times during the events open to any member of the public. To protect the privacy of the individuals involved, no identifying information has been used.

Website: JAntonPoetry.com
Instagram: @jantonpoetry
Facebook: J. Anton Poetry
Goodreads: J. Anton Davis

All Points Creative, LLC
P.O. Box 98232
Raleigh, North Carolina 27624

ISBN: 978-1-7355407-0-2 (Paperback)
ISBN: 978-1-7355407-1-9 (eBook)

To my wife, Alexandra,
the woman my heart was always searching for,

to our grandparents and parents,
whose marriages have taught us so much,

and

to the thousands of couples I was able to marry,
who shared with me their families, friends, and
wedding days, and who provided the memorable
moments that made this book possible.

Table of Contents

CONTENTS

I

S

LOVE
IS

A FORMER MAGISTRATE'S POETIC
REFLECTIONS ON LOVE AND
MARRIAGE IN A COUNTY
COURTHOUSE

Introduction

This is a book about love, specifically, the love that I witnessed during the nearly 6,000 civil wedding ceremonies I performed as a North Carolina Magistrate Judge from 2013 to 2019.

As the officiant of those many wedding ceremonies, my vantage point was not unlike that of a teacher at the head of a classroom. I was able to observe not only the couples I was marrying, but their family and friends, other wedding parties, and even law enforcement officers and individuals present for various criminal matters to be heard between ceremonies. I had a bird's-eye view of every kiss, cheer, tear, and smile. Understanding the uniqueness of my position, I decided early on that I would one day commit my experiences to writing so that others could envision what I saw and feel what I felt.

While there are countless stories I could share from those ceremonies – like the time a young child snuck up behind me and pushed the bright red security button on the underside of my bench, summoning a crowd of sheriff's deputies – this book focuses on the most memorable and powerful moments I witnessed.

There is something special about weddings, something that allows people to let their guards down and connect with others at a very deep, emotional level. As an officiant, even I had to keep from choking up at times. I can partially blame that reflex on my mom, who taught me from a young age that tears were made for beauty just as much as sadness. However, I think the greater provocateur of the raw, unfiltered emotions that I and many others feel at weddings is the simple, innocent, and evocative nature of the ceremony itself, one in which two people promise to love and honor each other for the rest of their lives.

The poems in this book describe only a fraction of the myriad unforgettable moments I witnessed in Courtroom 901 of the Wake County Justice Center in Raleigh, North Carolina. Those many wedding ceremonies have left an indelible mark on me. After reading these poems, I hope that you will feel the same.

LOVE

IS

A FORMER MAGISTRATE'S POETIC
REFLECTIONS ON LOVE AND
MARRIAGE IN A COUNTY
COURTHOUSE

Prologue

When I started writing these poems, my sister reminded me that not everyone has attended a courtroom wedding ceremony. Various references, she explained, would not make sense without some understanding of the civil wedding ceremony process. Out of a desire to not only be a good younger brother, but an intelligible poet, I will briefly explain the context within which my poems took place.

Every civil wedding ceremony is different. Not only did the structure of my ceremonies change over time and differ from that of my colleagues, every county and state in America likely has its own unique process. In general, however, every wedding ceremony I officiated included three steps.

First, each couple would approach the bench and present their wedding licenses and state wedding ceremony fee – it was actually the receipts I wrote for those fees that allowed me to keep a running tally of the nearly 6,000 ceremonies I performed during my time as a magistrate judge.

Second, I would explain the structure of the ceremony to the couple to be sure we were all on the same page before we began. I found that this prior explanation helped to relax those who were nervous. Please note, however, as I am sure many cellphone videos can confirm – to the glee of witnesses and the annoyance of newlyweds – when a person is in front of a courtroom full of people, the directions he or she has been given will often go straight out the window.

Third, I would lead the couple through the ceremony itself, made up of an introduction, the exchanging of vows and, if applicable, rings, and the pronouncement of marriage. The couple would then often take pictures with their two legal witnesses and the other members of their wedding party – sometimes I was in the pictures, sometimes I took them.

Within that broad structure, the countless weddings I performed varied greatly. As I also heard criminal matters in my courtroom, sometimes between one wedding ceremony and the next, couples could not reserve the room solely for their wedding party. Due to the fluid nature of the courtroom schedule, there were no signups for time slots, either. That meant that if five couples and all of their witnesses showed up at the same time, one couple would be married while four other wedding parties watched, often filling the courtroom.

While large crowds could sometimes lead to heightened nerves and increased tension among waiting parties, just as often it had the opposite effect; the courtroom turned into a place of shared celebration. It was always encouraging to see a courtroom full of strangers cheer for a new couple as they kissed at the pronouncement of marriage. Some newlyweds even lingered after their own ceremonies to celebrate the couple behind them, honoring the simple fidelity of acquaintance that had been born through the small talk exchanged in the moments between earlier ceremonies.

Wedding garb ran the gamut, from full wedding dresses to gym clothes, military fatigues, police uniforms, kilts, capes, tuxedos, and "I'm with him" tee shirts with an arrow pointing in the direction of the groom. Rings, which were not legally required, were made of yellow gold, white gold, silver, and silicone, candy, tattoo ink, cloth, and flowers.

Couples arrived with forty witnesses, two witnesses, and no witnesses at all. Those without witnesses often enlisted the help of other wedding parties. However, on especially slow wedding days, couples often tied the knot with the signatures of a criminal defendant and a defense attorney, both of whom had been recruited while waiting outside of some soon-to-be-opened courtroom floors below.

Every ceremony was different, shaped by the lives and love of those participating, a point that I hope each poem in this book will reinforce as you read.

Please enjoy these stories and the beautiful gestures, memories, and marriages they describe.

L

Love is shaking

Love is
shaking,
fumbling, mumbling,
and stuttering.

It is
dropped rings,
forgotten lines,
and runny noses.

Love is
preparing
a speech
or song
and being
too emotional
to deliver it.

It is
smeared makeup,
transferred lipstick,
and forgotten paperwork.

We think that love
has smooth,
straight edges,
that it is devoid
of imperfections,
but it has never been that,
and only at its worst,

most hollow point
would it appear so.

Love is climbing

Love is
climbing
eight flights of stairs
to meet your bride
because you have
an intense fear
of elevators.

It is
showing up sweaty
and out of breath
from the ascent,
without a trace
of bitterness
or annoyance,
but only joy
and excitement.

Love is
your bride
receiving you
into her arms
without a hint
of judgment
or embarrassment,
but with an expression
of unwavering pride,
one that is strengthened,
not weakened,
by the path you took
to stand beside her.

Love is pretending

Love is
pretending
you left the rings
at home
when the judge
asks you to present them,
just to see
the expression
on her face
when she realizes
you have tricked her.

It is
pausing
longer than anyone should
before saying, "I do,"
simply to see the relief
in his eyes
when he realizes
that not only does his bride
have a sense of humor,
but she has promised
to spend her life with him,
a truth which contradicts
the panicked thoughts
he felt only moments before.

Love is
playing
together

in the exhilarating,
fearful, hopeful,
and worthy
game of life,
holding each other
on the difficult days
and laughing together
on the days
that move so fast
precisely because
you never
want them to end.

It is
removing
the protections
you have developed
throughout your life
to withstand
the barbs
of your fellow man,
returning to
the simplicity
and silliness
of childhood,
if only with one person,
enjoying together
a rare and powerful
respite
from a guarded
and wary world.

Love is crying

Love is
crying
as you state
your vows,
a perfect contrast
to the look
you projected
upon entering
the courtroom,
one of a man
wholly unaffected
by the magnitude
or beauty
of the ceremony
to come.

It is
transitioning
from exaggerated confidence
to a quivering lip
and a rolling tear,
from appearing aloof and stoic
to wiping puffy eyes
and a runny nose.

Love is
shedding
your steely facade,
realizing it is
not strong enough

to resist
the warm,
disarming smile
of your bride,
and it is
growing
to understand
that such a barrier
only succeeds in creating
unnecessary
and undesirable
distance.

Love is holding

Love is
holding
a crying child
as you exchange
vows and rings,
at once promising
to share your life
with another,
as long as you live,
while simultaneously
acknowledging
and comforting
the sweet soul
in your arms
who wants assurance
that she will not
be lost
in the shuffle
of changing
family dynamics.

It is
foregoing
any hope
that this will be
merely "your day,"
exchanging that concept for one
of communal celebration,
unity, and self-sacrifice.

Love is
providing
young eyes
with a close-up view
of the tears shed,
the kiss shared,
and the love declared
by both you
and your spouse,
burning a sublime
and indelible image
of family
into an innocent
and impressionable mind.

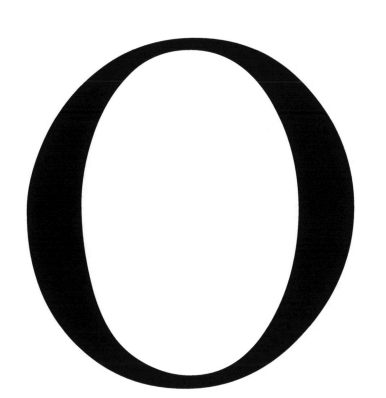

Love is singing

Love is
singing
joyfully
with family
and friends,
sharing
the bright melodies
of your native tongue,
the syllables as vibrant
and colorful
as the patterns
on your clothes.

It is
dancing
together,
both young and old,
to celebrate the wedding
of two members
of a proud community,
whose sincere
and unabashed smiles
embody
the jubilation
of the entire group.

Love is
yielding
to the many witnesses
pulling you into

the happy chaos,
your momentary hesitation
betraying
a humble reluctance
to be the center of attention,
even on your wedding day.

It is
wondering
how life
would even be possible
without such a steadfast
and devoted community
surrounding you,
while knowing
that you will never
have to find out.

Love is watching

Love is
watching
your daughter's wedding
from the other side
of the world,
crying the whole time
into an unmuted microphone,
providing much needed
comic relief
for a jittery couple.

It is
searching
for a signal
until you hear
the same voice
that used to wake you
in the morning,
leading to cheers
from a worried courtroom
and a confident nod
from a child now ready
to put on one final show
for mom and dad.

Love is
crowding
around a phone
to laugh and blow kisses,
switching back and forth

between English
and your first language
so that your parents
and new husband
can congratulate
one another.

It is
condensing
the vastness
of the earth
into a single room,
suspending
time and space
in order to soothe
the incurable ache
of distance
between you
and those who
understand most
the many twists
and turns
that have brought you
to this day.

Love is capes

Love is
capes,
tuxedo tees,
and May the 4th,
lightsaber bouquets
and tattoo rings.

It is
his and hers,
king and queen,
Mickey and Minnie,
and "I'm with him."

Love is
showing the world
that you, quirks and all,
have found someone
who understands you,
who speaks your language,
and who asks only
that you be yourself,
a request to which
you have so gladly
consented.

Love is cheering

Love is
cheering
for perfect strangers
as they kiss
at the pronouncement
of marriage,
not because
they look like you,
sound like you,
or think like you,
but solely because
you are witnessing
the beautiful,
vulnerable,
climactic giving
of one life
to another.

Love is aging

Love is
aging
in reverse
at the touch
of a hand
and the kiss
of a cheek,
a greeting
between two
adventurers
in the magnificent
sunset of life.

It is
wading,
once again,
into the nourishing waters
of lifelong companionship,
making that promise
with as much
joy and sincerity
as the first time
you did so,
a promise
that was kept
to the end.

Love is
uniting
a youthful spirit

and a weathered body,
finding another
who shares the same
peculiar paradox,
and embarking together
into the great unknown.

Love is surprising

Love is
surprising
your fiancée
with a ring
she didn't expect,
knowing
as you placed it
on her finger
that she was thrilled
to marry you
when there was
no ring at all.

It is
preparing vows,
unbeknownst
to your bride,
speaking of
your first date,
the many struggles
you have overcome
together,
and the joyful days
that lie ahead.

Love is
organizing
a video stream
with your bride's family
without telling her

beforehand,
allowing her parents
and siblings to "attend"
the ceremony,
cheering and crying
as if they were
in the front pew.

It is
beautiful,
exciting,
honoring,
and innocent,
youthful,
playful,
mischievous,
and fun.

Love is finding

Love is
finding
that person
you once knew,
the one who helped you
build sandcastles
and catch fireflies,
who rode bikes with you
through the neighborhood
and shared snacks with you
at the pool.

It is
discovering
that no matter
the years
that have passed,
each filled
with countless
unshared memories,
the touch
of her hand
is as familiar
and comforting
as if you had
held it all along.

Love is
reclaiming
an innocent affection,

born at a time
when life was simpler
and the world
weighed less.

It is
returning
to an adventure
once lost
to the ages.

Love is saving

Love is
saving
every penny you have
just to buy
a wedding license
and five minutes
of court time.

It is a man
of humble means,
bursting with pride
at the beauty
before him,
and a bride
whose eyes and smile
shine brighter
than the ring
she will not receive.

Love is
rejoicing
simply in the unity
of marriage, a bond
measured in kisses,
not carats.

Love is committing

Love is
committing
to someone
in a crisp uniform,
knowing you are
now partners
in a great calling,
one built upon
sacrifice,
giving,
"be safe"s,
and "come home"s.

It is
presenting
silicone rings
instead of metallic ones,
as gold and silver
can snag easily
on a battlefield
or in a patrol car.

Love is
treasuring
each moment together,
never having the luxury
of forgetting
that life is short,
a truth which magnifies
the tenderness

of a goodnight kiss
and the sweetness
of a waking smile,
a few of the many
small moments
that make the hours,
days, and months apart
worth every second.

Love is welcoming

Love is
welcoming
the child
of your bride
into your life
with the same
enthusiasm
as you welcome
her mother.

It is
presenting
two rings
on your wedding day
instead of one,
because you brought
a second
to show an innocent,
young soul
that she would not be
begrudgingly accepted
into your life,
included merely as a part
of a package deal,
but would be eagerly
and intentionally chosen
to be yours
to guide and protect
for the rest
of your life.

Love is
a couple
joined together
by the hands
of a child
who looks from one
to the other
as they declare
their mutual devotion,
understanding
even at a young age
that her place
in this new relationship
is real and absolute,
even tangibly manifested
in a most solemn ceremony.

In a world
often brimming
with selfishness
and stingy affections,
love is
a most devastating
force.

E

Love is sharing

Love is
sharing
your bouquet
with the next bride,
wanting her "big day"
to be as wonderful
and memorable
as your own.

It is
handing
twenty dollars
to a wide-eyed couple
that just realized
they forgot the wedding fee,
politely waving away
their offers of repayment.

Love is
transforming
from newlyweds
into photographers,
happily capturing
the memories
of a couple
you have never met
and will never see again,
hugging and crying
together
as if lifelong friends.

It is
self-forgetting,
light, joyful,
and communal,
welcoming,
supportive,
encouraging,
and ennobling.

Love is supporting

Love is
supporting
each other,
not only
in sickness
and in health,
but at home
and abroad.

It is
joining
with another
to brave
the transition
between all
you have ever known
and all
you have never known,
embarking together
on the great
challenges of life
while far from
the safety nets
of extended family
and familiar systems.

Love is
leaping
hand in hand
into a new world
with the person

who makes you feel
as if you never left home.

Love is bowing

Love is
bowing
to touch the feet
of your elders,
humbling yourself
to honor those
whose hearts
first held the hope
of your marriage.

It is
understanding
that while a wedding
is a special event
for you, the couple,
there are many
who have shaped you
and brought you
to this day
who have as much
cause to celebrate
as you yourself.

Love is
welcoming
others
into your marriage,
sharing a sweet cookie
of celebration
and cheerfully hugging

the colorfully clad
and endlessly wise sages
who will support you
as you dare to uphold
your lofty vows.

Love is jumping

Love is
jumping
the broom
at the request
of a grandparent,
celebrating in the manner
of your ancestors,
not because you have to,
as they did,
but because you choose to,
honoring their memories
and the small joys
they were able to find
amidst the scourge
of American slavery.

It is
celebrating
the start
of a joyful,
lifelong relationship
in the bright lights
of a county courtroom,
exercising the right
to share your union
openly with the world,
a right that is fitting
of a ceremony
so moving and evocative,
a right that countless couples

were so callously denied
for generations.

Love is
remembering
and acknowledging
what your wedding means,
not only to you,
but to all who came before you,
those whose secret unions
are now remembered
and celebrated
with your own.

Love is *Loving*

Love is
Loving
v. Virginia,
manifested
over and over again
in the weddings
of innumerable
interracial couples,
kissing at the pronouncement
of a once-criminalized union.

It is
rejecting
the distorted belief
that skin color
holds an
incontestable veto
in matters
of the heart.

Love is
showing
the world
that marriage
and family
stand upon
much firmer foundations
than what one may observe
with the naked eye,
that both rest upon

the unshakeable
and hallowed ground
of mutual, sincere,
and mysterious
affection.

Love is silence

Love is
silence
in a courtroom
full of people,
save for
an awestruck judge
reading vows
and the rustle
of clothing
from the quick,
precise hand movements
of an interpreter.

It is
tears, smiles,
and a kiss,
cheered
by a sea
of waving hands
and emphatic gestures
of congratulations.

Love is
finding
someone who speaks
your language,
no matter its rarity,
and spending
the rest of your life
carving love letters

into the space
between you.

Love is waiting

Love is
waiting
decades
to publicly celebrate
a lifelong commitment,
a relationship
that has weathered
pain and sorrow,
celebrations and triumphs,
and all manner
of challenges.

It is
standing
before your bride,
shaking,
even though
you have held her hands
ten thousand times,
trading rings
that have only been removed
to be put back on.

Love is
accepting
the long-denied opportunity
to stand where you are,
showing no signs of bitterness
at the delay,
focused only

on your partner,
punctuating in law
what was established in life
many years ago.

Love is remembering

Love is
remembering
what led you
to marry
that person
in the first place,
the first time,
when your bond
was untested
and had yet
to be broken.

It is
returning
after many
lessons learned
to reunite
with the one
you thought
you might never
see again,
weeping now
because of the beautiful gift
that is forgiveness,
because you know
with a weathered wisdom
the commitment
you now make,
understanding fully
the awesome weight

of the sacrifice
it will demand of you
and yet still desiring
to bind yourself
once more.

Love is
the small flower
that breaches
the scorched earth
after a forest fire,
fragile and unassuming,
yet holding within itself
the power to cover
the whole world
if it might only endure.

Love is refusing

Love is
refusing
to let a diagnosis
dictate your life,
choosing still
to invite and answer
that most solemn question,
"as long
as you both
shall live?"

It is
a bride
wearing
a stylish bandana
as she says
"I do,"
and a groom
looking into her eyes
with the care
of a true partner,
one who
has fulfilled
the weighty demands
of his wedding vows
a hundred times
before stating them.

Love is
ascending

to new heights
of bravery
and unity
in the face
of life's greatest specter,
affirming the truth
that though fear is
a tsunami, love is
an impenetrable fortress.

Love is spending

Love is
spending
a year
marrying hundreds
of other couples,
dreaming
all the while
about adding
one more ring
to your finger,
waiting also
to receive my own.

It is
surprising
me in court
with a coffee
and your smile,
sitting quietly
on the back pew
until everyone was gone,
coming forward then
so that we could talk,
even if only
for a short time
and at a distance,
consequences
of our attempt
to represent well
our shared

and honorable
profession.

Love is
hanging
my robe
in the courtroom closet
the last time
before our wedding day,
exhaling
almost to tears,
knowing that we had
finally made it,
that it was our turn
to trade vows,
rings, and kisses.

It is
watching
you walk
down the aisle,
your beauty in white
matched only
by your loveliness
in every other color,
your magnificence
in a dress
rivaled only
by your radiance
in blue jeans,
gym shorts,
and sweatpants.

Love is
us,
sharing
the twists
and turns
of our lives,
infinitely stronger
together
than the sum
of our separate parts,
committed until death,
where I will take with me
the ring on my finger
as my most prized possession,
bragging to all
who will listen
that, yes, it was that
incredible woman
with whom
I shared my life.

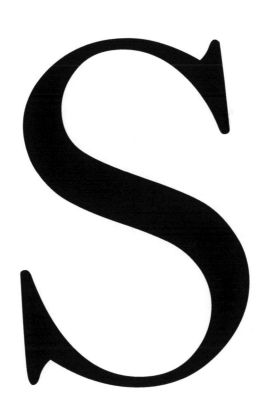

Acknowledgements

Publishing this book of poems is one of the most fulfilling things I have ever done. I want to thank everyone, named and unnamed, who helped me to reach the finish line.

Thank you to my wife, Alexandra, who was not only a source of great encouragement throughout this process, but who was an incredible editor and who has taught me throughout our marriage that goals – even artistic ones – are reached only by showing up, day in and day out, to do the hard work set before you.

Thank you to my father, John, who was the first true artist I ever met. He was an honest critic throughout multiple drafts of these poems and this book, providing me with the blunt, yet encouraging, feedback of someone who knows what it is to create and to put your work out into the world.

ACKNOWLEDGEMENTS

Thank you to my mother, Kathy, who has always been my biggest cheerleader. She taught me how to see the world as this book describes it, one rich with emotion and depth. The text message that she sent me after reading the first proof copy of *Love is* had so many exclamation points and explanations of sobbing during certain poems that I felt I had nothing left to prove to any other reader.

Thank you to my mother-in-law, Laurie, and my father-in-law, Ed, for their edits, feedback, and genuine excitement about this project. Their wisdom and thoughtful guidance have helped me to keep my head on straight throughout this process.

Thank you to my friend, editor, and book designer, Dillon Lunn, for the hours he spent working on this project. He worked with me for months on an unrelated book, just for me to eventually tell him that I had a brand new idea that I wanted to pursue first. Dillon's interest and support never wavered and the expertise he shared with me, developed

ACKNOWLEDGEMENTS

from publishing his first novel, *The Kingdom vs John Reid*, was invaluable.

Thank you to my sister, Lauren, for her thoughtful and honest critiques. As an actress and film buff, she has a deep understanding of presentation and audiences. She was the first person who explained to me that the order and grouping of my poems was almost as important as the words themselves.

Thank you to my many beta readers. Their thoughts and input helped add the polish to this book that I desperately wanted to see before it was published.

Thank you to the sheriff's deputies, clerks, magistrates, judges, attorneys, registers of deeds, and everyone else who helped make the thousands of weddings I performed possible. Their friendship and encouragement helped get me through even the longest days at the office.

Follow the Author

Keep up with the writings of J. Anton Davis by following these five steps:

- ➤ Visit his website, JAntonPoetry.com.
- ➤ Sign up for the J. Anton Poetry e-Newsletter.
- ➤ Follow @jantonpoetry on Instagram.
- ➤ Like the J. Anton Poetry Facebook page.
- ➤ Email him at JAntonPoetry@gmail.com to let him know what you thought of *Love is*.

If you enjoyed this book, remember to leave a review on Amazon.com and Goodreads.com. Also, don't forget to tell your friends, family, and social media connections about it, and let your local bookstores know that you would like to see works by J. Anton Davis on their shelves.

Thank you for reading!

ISBN: 978-1-7355407-0-2 (Paperback)
ISBN: 978-1-7355407-1-9 (eBook)

Author Biography

J. Anton Davis is a husband, father, attorney, and poet. A born-and-raised North Carolinian, he lives in Raleigh with his wife, Alexandra, and son, James.

Though Davis has written poetry and fiction privately for 20 years, he launched his website, JAntonPoetry.com, in 2019 to begin sharing his writing publicly. His poems focus on the deep meaning hidden within the seemingly insignificant and mundane.

Beyond writing poetry and fiction, Davis enjoys exploring local Greenway trails, playing soccer, and spending time with his family and friends.

J. Anton, James, and Alexandra Davis
August, 2020

Your Own Poetry

_____

_____

_____

_____

_____

_____

_____

_____

_____

_____

_____

_____

_____

_____

_____

_____

_____

_____

_____

_____

Your Own Poetry

Your Own Poetry

Your Own Poetry

Your Own Poetry

Your Own Poetry

_____

_____

_____

_____

_____

_____

_____

_____

_____

_____

_____

_____

_____

_____

_____

_____

_____

_____

_____

_____

_____

_____

_____

_____

Made in the USA
Columbia, SC
25 September 2020

21529644R00050